LOOKING AFTER BABY

JULIE PARMENTER

REDCLIFFE
Bristol

First published in 1993 for
Children of the Nineties
University of Bristol by
Redcliffe Press Ltd, Bristol

© *Children of the Nineties*

ISBN 1 872971 74 1

British Library Cataloguing-in-Publication Data.
A catalogue record for this book is available
from the British Library.

Typeset and printed by The Longdunn Press Ltd., Bristol

Contents

ACKNOWLEDGEMENTS

I would like to thank all those mothers who joined this study and all staff at Children of the Nineties for their support and encouragement. I would also like to give special thanks to the following people for their help: Professor J. Golding, Dr. R. Smith, Mr R. Bateman, Mr D. Carmichael and Mr S. Colmer.
The following gave their kind permission for the reproduction of photographs in this book: Bristol Evening Post & Western Daily Press, Oxford University Press, LRP Ltd., Wyeth Nutrition and The Home Companion.

Illustrations by Catherine Goodsman.

Introduction

The twentieth century has seen many changes in advice to mothers on how to care for their infants. This advice has moved from the rigid clock-watching of the 1940s and '50s to the slightly more relaxed guidelines of the 1960s, and to the permissive demand feeding/sleeping of the 1970s and '80s.

At Bristol University a long-term study is being made of pregnancy and childhood, which we have called the 'Children of the Nineties'.

As many people are now aware, guidance on the sleeping position of babies has changed completely in recent years. As part of the advice on safeguarding against cot death (Sudden Infant Death Syndrome) it is now recommended that babies are placed on their back to sleep. Through analysis of the Children of the Nineties data it was clear that Avon mothers had taken the 'Back to Sleep' message to heart and the sleep position of babies in the Avon area underwent a striking change from tummy sleeping to back sleeping.

This started us thinking about other baby care messages and advice, how they are accepted or rejected by parents and how other things may have affected the care of babies over the years.

Using the Avon area and the Children of the Nineties study as a base, we invited other mothers who had given birth in Avon at any time from 1950–1989 to join a new part of the main study. We call this part 'Yesterday, Today . . . Tomorrow'. Mothers who enrolled were sent a questionnaire asking them how they cared for each baby and how they felt baby care has changed over the years. The results of that study are presented here, along with accounts of what the 'experts' said and indeed say.

This is not a new baby care manual. But we hope it highlights the changes in advice given over the years and show what mothers actually have done and do in caring for their babies. The history of baby care advice cannot be a substitute for a modern day baby care manual. However, as Christina Hardyment stated in her work on the subject, it can be an 'essential antidote' to all the conflicting and confusing opinions that a new mother is subjected to.

This is our antidote to the sometimes indigestible ingredients of the 'perfect baby' recipe.

Is Breast Best?

The decline in breast feeding this century can be seen as a part of the general emancipation of women, which began in the 1920s along with 'short hair, short skirts, contraceptives and cigarettes.'[1] However, the message that breast milk is best milk has been relayed by health care 'experts' since Hippocrates – 'One's own milk is beneficial, others harmful'[2] – but human mothers have always found an alternative method of feeding their young. The development of sophisticated formula milk and feeding equipment this century has only made artificial feeding safer. The manufacturers answered a need, they did not invent the practice.

The interwar years saw the 'Breast Is Best' banner taken up by the New Zealand doctor, Sir Frederick Truby King. His lecture tours of England did much, not only to encourage mothers to breast feed their babies, but also to develop good hygienic practice in bottle feeding. Nature has always been, and remains, a powerful advertising theme and so were religious images at that time. Although society was becoming increasingly secular, the image of the baby Jesus at his mother's breast was often used to promote the practice of breast feeding.

The first words to greet a mother seeking advice from the Truby King baby manual on feeding are from Milton:

'Accuse not Nature, she hath done her part;
Do but thine.'[3]

There went the 'excuse' of Nature not providing enough milk! It was a mother's duty to ensure that she was healthy and strong and therefore capable of producing 'the only perfect food' for her baby. There was a strong emphasis on 'duty' for all members of society at this time. The ideas on rearing children were rooted in promoting a sense of duty and discipline. Truby King makes that very clear:

'A woman's milk is not her own. It is created for the baby, and the first duty of the mother is to ensure, by foresight, a proper supply of the only perfect food – the baby's birthright.'[4]

Despite the emphasis on infant health and the appeal to a mother's 'natural' sense of duty, the 1930s are still debated by historians as hungry or healthy? Although infant death rates continued to drop, their decline was slower between 1931 and 1941 than at any other time since 1900. In fact, the infant death rate fell faster during each of the two World Wars than at any time previously – giving credence to the idea that war is good for babies! Of course there are many factors but at a time when antibiotics were in their infancy, there can be no doubt that methods of infant feeding made a contribution to the overall infant mortality rates. The official statistics offered a rather optimistic view of the nation's health. In 1931 individual areas in large cities, such as Manchester, contained huge variations in standards of health. One district reported an infant death rate of 44 per thousand, while another reported 143 per thousand.[5] There were similar variations between the social classes. Whilst it is not reasonable to suggest that universal breast feeding would have solved these differences, it was known that breast feeding gives valuable protection against disease to the vulnerable new born infant, at a time when bottle feeding was less hygienic than today.

The medical profession has been remarkably consistent in its advice on breast feeding throughout the years – Breast feeding is Best Feeding has always been the message. Why then do women consistently ignore it? The idea that it could be difficult to breast feed does not fit with the message that it is a perfectly 'natural' thing to do. If we hear the word 'natural' we tend to think that whatever it is applied to is easy. For many women breast feeding is a natural, easy process, but for others it is a painful, unpleasant and frustrating business that brings feelings of guilt and inadequacy when it fails.

Just as wet nurses were a 'necessary evil' to the medical profession two centuries ago, with rules and regulations for their employment being put forward as an exercise in damage limitation, now it is the turn of bottle feeding. Sir Truby King remained totally opposed and when the mother turns to his text she finds that 'Before describing artificial feeding it is desirable to state emphatically that no system of bottle feeding can ever give to either mother or child the advantages which both derive from suckling . . . imitation cannot be made identical with the original, and must always be inferior to it.'[6] He grudgingly allows that 'every infant who cannot be suckled in the natural way is entitled to receive properly modified milk'.[7]

It is not until 1946 that Dr. Spock, the next child care 'expert', gives guarded permission to guilt-ridden, bottle feeding mothers. Whilst defending breast feeding as a more natural and safer method of feeding he allows that in the end a baby needs a 'cheerful mother more than he needs breast milk.'[8] The *Motherhood Book*, another popular text for parents in the 1940s, felt it to be a 'tragedy' when 'ignorance, fear and mismanagement' denied a baby his 'rightful food'.[9] Nurse Crawford, writing in *Mother* magazine in May 1951, states that 'To breast feed your baby if you are able is a duty as well as a joy to you both.'[10]

Therefore mothers who chose to bottle feed their infants approached the 1950s with a firmly established sense of guilt. Yet bottle feeding still flourished. Spock believed the reason to be the improvement in bottle feeding equipment and the quality of formula milk, plus 'peer group' pressure and fashion. Spock spoke to the mothers in the 1950s, Wallace spoke to those who advised the mothers. Wallace's text book for nursery nurses (1951) accepted only one reason for not attempting to breast feed: the presence of a serious organic disease such as tuberculosis in the mother. One mother in the Yesterday, Today . . . Tomorrow study was advised not to breast feed her first three children because she suffered from tuberculosis in her teens. With her fourth child she says 'I wanted to try so I just went ahead and I enjoyed it and wished I had fed the others'.

While finding reassurance about bottle feeding from Spock, mothers were lectured on breast feeding by the nursing staff they came into contact with. We asked the Yesterday, Today . . . Tomorrow study to give their reasons for choosing to breast or bottle feed. The response from the breast feeding mothers of the 1950s varied from 'It was the natural thing to do' to 'It was compulsory when you were in hospital'.

Several baby care magazines were in circulation at this time for both mothers and health care professionals. In all there are to be found articles promoting breast feeding, usually written by a nurse, midwife or doctor alongside strong advertisements for formula milk. Nurse Crawford writes that 'every healthy mother should try and feed her baby herself', advice endorsed by the Ostermilk advertisement in the same magazine. 'It (Ostermilk) is the ideal alternative when mothers cannot breast feed their babies'. There is the added incentive of a 'sweet temper, peaceful nights and healthy gains'. Trufood advertising in *Mother & Child*, 1951, adopts the same style with even more back-handed promotion of breast feeding. 'Of course I'll feed my baby myself. Because I know MY milk will give him the best start in life and help protect him against illness. I don't expect any difficulties and if I DO have any, my doctor will help me. But, if I REALLY can't breast feed I'll be thankful for Trufood.'

Writing in the same magazine, Dr. Wilson laments the lack of breast feeding and feels that if the 'time, expense and energy' directed at bottle feeding were extended to breast feeding there would be no need for articles such as his. In Woolwich in 1947 80% of mothers were still breast feeding their babies at six months. Dr. Wilson wonders why, if this can be done in one area by an efficient and cooperative team, it is not being done everywhere? Why indeed? It was not being achieved in Bristol. Ross and Herdan, writing for the Glaxo report 1953, produced breast feeding figures for Bristol babies in 1949: at three months only 36% of mothers were still breast feeding.

Dr. Wilson is unconvinced by 'excuses' such as crowded living conditions and housing difficulties. Of the Yesterday, Today . . . Tomorrow study mothers 16% were living with their parents when their first child was born in the 1950s. A further 15% were living in rented rooms. Several of the mothers commented that their home conditions were not suitable for breast feeding – 'younger brothers and sisters around the house'; 'little or no privacy'. There was certainly very little peace and quiet for the new, inexperienced mother in cramped living conditions. Bristol, as with other large cities in Britain in the 1950s, faced a housing crisis and even though hindsight tells us that the creation of large housing estates brought more problems than they solved, at the time they gave much needed, modern accommodation to young families – even if it was over a hundred feet above ground!

Feeding Method
1950

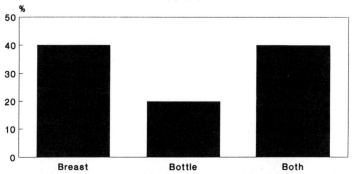

Duration of Feeding
1950

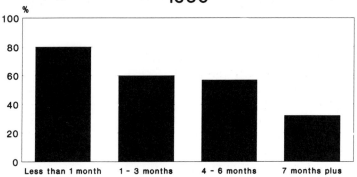

In the Yesterday, Today . . . Tomorrow study, of 176 children born in the 1950s, 40% were breast fed only and 40% were breast and bottle fed. In total 80% received breast milk at some stage and 32% of those were still breast fed at seven months.

The comments made by many of the study mothers show that bottle feeding their babies was not always a matter of choice but of necessity:

'I tried very hard to breast feed, there just wasn't any milk.'

'Multiple breast abscess led to a major operation and I could not feed any of my children.'

'I was ill myself and the nurse stopped me.'

YTT Study mothers of the 1950s.

The 1960s saw a decline in breast feeding nationally and Bristol was no exception. In total 255 study children were born in the 1960s, and the following tables give details about their breast feeding patterns.

Overall 65% of babies had been breast fed. This is a large decline from the 80% of the 1950s. If we look at the duration of breast feeding there is also a decline in those who were still breast feeding at seven months from 32% to 16%.

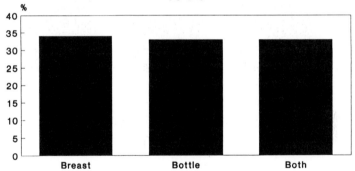

Feeding method
1960

The problem was not so much getting mothers to breast feed initially but persuading them to continue to breast feed once they left the 'compulsory' atmosphere of the hospital. The Newsoms' study of Nottingham mothers and babies in 1963 revealed the same problem:

'Four days after birth 83% of mothers are either breast feeding or at least still making some attempt to do so. However, it is clear from what they say that a large number of them only do this because they believe or have been told

Duration of Feeding
1960

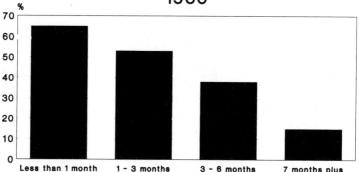

that it is expected of them. They have little intention of
carrying on once they get out of hospital.'[11]

The late 1960s and early 1970s saw breast feeding decline to an all
time low nationally. The dramatic difference in the 1970s when
compared to the previous two decades lies in those who started to breast
feed at all, 80% in the 1950s, 65% in the 1960s and 51% in the 1970s.

Reviewing the comments made by YTT study mothers of the 1970s
a new element has to be taken into consideration. They simply did not
want to breast feed, did not like the idea of it and also that they were
not encouraged to do so.

'Dr. present at birth did not believe in starting with breast
and changing to bottle so I opted for bottle.'
'Breast feeding was not fashionable in the early '70s, bottle
feeding was encouraged.'
'Hospital said it was better to bottle feed, he was a slow
feeder.'
'I was not given any help or encouragement to breast feed in
hospital, they had no time for me.'
YTT Study Mothers 1970s.

This reveals quite a striking change of attitude from 'compulsory'
breast feeding to a rather laid back, 'anything goes' policy. The DHSS
Report on Health and Social Subjects 1974 strongly recommends
breast feeding.

'We are concerned that women do not always receive
adequate advice and encouragement to breast feed their
babies.'[12]

While it is tempting to lay the blame for the national decline in
breast feeding on one particular body – namely the health care

10

Feeding Method
1970

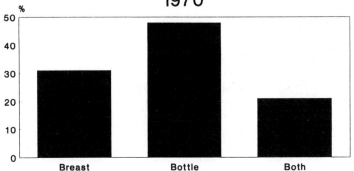

Duration of Feeding
1970

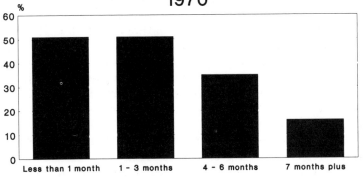

professionals, especially as they are the common denominator that all pregnant women and nursing mothers will have contact with at some time – there are many other factors to take into consideration.

There is no doubt that the commercialisation of formula milk had grown and developed to the point where although breast feeding may have given a relative advantage to babies, it was no longer seen as an absolute necessity for health. The Newsoms give the rise of the 'cult of the breast' as another explanation. Its role as a public sexual symbol at this time led to confusion and embarrassment over the function of the breast. In this study only 2% of mothers of the 1970s gave embarrassment as a reason for giving up breast feeding, and none stated that they gave up because their husbands disliked it, although these may well have been reasons why mothers did not attempt to breast feed at all.

Another assumption for the decline has been the growing number of mothers returning to work, but there is a great deal of empirical evidence that refutes this. The British Birth Survey of 1970 found that maternal employment was not a factor in feeding trends. If anything breast feeding affected maternal employment patterns positively and not vice versa. In this study only 20% of the 1970s study mothers returned to work at all. The factors that seem to determine attitudes toward long term breast feeding are the mothers' educational and social status.

Child Development as a subject taught in secondary education has been on the time table only since the late 1970s and then only in the most progressive schools. Although it is a common subject in schools now it is still taught on an optional basis and chosen mainly by girls. Previously young girls may have been taught a little about preparing baby food in a domestic science class. Parenting as such remains a job that is assumed to need no qualifications or study. Often the only information a new mother has about her new job is whatever the midwife tells her at clinic and whatever her mother, sister or friend have to contribute. Her success in breast feeding will depend on the attitudes she, and her partner, acquire.

Attitudes can be carefully and gently cultivated, but few mothers respond well to bullying and dictation, and the post-war need for firm direction that Truby King and indeed Spock had fulfilled so well was now gone. Instead of being told what to do, people came to seek reassurance that what they chose to do was right. While bottle feeding mothers were assured that they were perfectly correct in their choice, those who were struggling to breast feed, to overcome engorged, painful breasts, cracked, bleeding nipples and other horrors of breast feeding were effectively demoralised. Why go through all that physical and emotional pain when you can make up a bottle?

Andrew and Penny Stanway went a long way to solving the breast versus bottle dilemma with their popular work *Breast Is Best* (1978). They advocated mixed feeding, feeding on demand, feeding to routine, feeding any which way you wanted to as long as it suited your and the baby's needs. Pure demand feeding can cause problems if your baby demands every two hours but on the whole the rigidity of four hourly feeding became much more relaxed and so did mothers. Perhaps the sure and steady increase in breast feeding rates, both initially and longer term, throughout the 1980s, as seen here in these graphs, could be the result of the more relaxed attitude.

50% of all the study children who were breast fed at all were still being breast fed at seven months, a very positive increase from the 16% of the 1970s. Baby care 'experts' were less insistent about breast

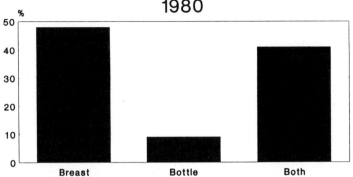

Feeding Method
1980

%

50	
40	
30	
20	
10	
0	

Breast   Bottle   Both

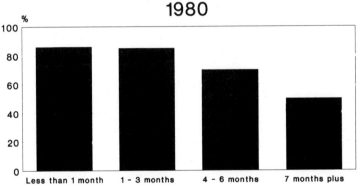

Duration of Feeding
1980

%

100	
80	
60	
40	
20	
0	

Less than 1 month   1 - 3 months   4 - 6 months   7 months plus

feeding, preferring to congratulate mothers who could and reassure mothers who could not. Jolly's *Book of Child Care* (1977) recommended that mothers should make a decision before the birth and be firm about it, so that they would not be pushed into a decision during their hospital stay. Cobb's *Babyshock* (1980) states that the only deciding factor to consider in choosing a method of feeding is whether the mother actually wants to breast feed. In this all the experts are of the same opinion – a mother must be willing to breast feed. Its success depends on her state of mind. This, however, puts unfair strain on the mother, for if breast feeding fails because of sore, bleeding nipples for example, it won't matter how willing she is to continue to breast feed. It will be a physical impossibility and only the most determined will cope with the hand expressing of milk and healing process to try again.

13

Although there are many reasons for cracked nipples, a major factor is the position of the baby. As stated earlier breast feeding is not actually an easy thing to do and get right, a baby who is not properly 'fixed' on to the breast will suckle on whatever he does have in his mouth, and if it is only the end of the nipple he is likely to damage it. Sally Inch stated that in 1987 fewer than 50% of mothers received help from a midwife at their first feeding attempt. Her paper 'Midwives in disarray?' questions the midwives' perception of their role in the breast feeding debate. *Midwifery Dialogue* (June 1991) carries an article discussing the pros and cons of breast feeding, its author F. Entwistle identifying the key points that need to be addressed for successful breast feeding.

Attitudes – especially those linked with sexuality and breast feeding.

Individual, professional help with feeding.

Good liaison between hospital and community services and the support of voluntary services such as the National Childbirth Trust.

In the same journal there is a full page advertisement for Farley's Ostermilk inviting midwives to visit their stand at the Royal College of Midwives Conference!

Breast feeding does not have any direct commercial value, we may or may not see the benefits in the health of future generations. *The Mail on Sunday* newspaper of September 27th 1992 offers 'conclusive proof that maternal milk builds healthier babies'. The *Mail's* source, an American study conducted at the University of Tennessee, has provided evidence that breast fed babies have a higher intellect and

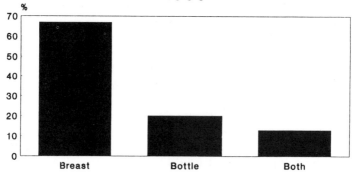

Feeding Method
1990

Duration of Feeding
1990

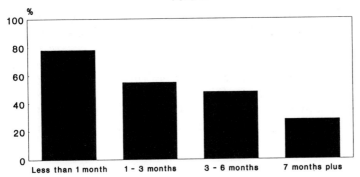

better eyesight than their bottle fed contemporaries. The Children of the Nineties study itself will throw more light on the differences between children who were breast or bottle fed – if there are any differences. At present 55% of mothers in the study were still breast feeding their babies at one month, 28% at six months.

The World Health Organisation began a worldwide campaign to promote breast feeding in 1989. That promotion has become known as 'The Baby Friendly Initiative' and every facility that provides maternity services has been invited to join the programme. There are ten steps that have to be undertaken and maintained.

Every facility providing maternity services and care for newborn infants should:

1. Have a written breast feeding policy that is routinely communicated to all health care staff.
2. Train all health care staff in skills necessary to implement this policy.
3. Inform all pregnant women about the benefits and management of breast feeding.
4. Help mothers initiate breast feeding within half an hour of birth.
5. Show mothers how to breast feed, and how to maintain lactation, even if they should be separated from their infants.
6. Give newborn infants no food or drink other than breast milk, unless medically indicated.
7. Practice rooming-in – allow mothers and infants to remain together – 24 hours a day.

15

8. Encourage breast feeding on demand.
9. Give no artificial teats or pacifiers (also called dummies or soothers) to breast feeding infants.
10. Foster the establishment of breast feeding support groups and refer mothers to them on discharge from the hospital or clinic.

The whole scheme has been designed to 'protect, promote and support breast feeding'.

Although these hospital initiatives will probably work very well, where the difficulties lie and have always lain is in the continuation of breast feeding in the community. Gallagher in her study *Infants, Mothers and Doctors* in Kentucky 1978 states that for mothers to breast feed successfully they have to have a fundamental belief in the process – which leads us back to education. Despite the sharp decline in the late 1960s and early 1970s in this country, the rise in breast feeding in the last 20 years has been substantial, with the health care profession, education and individual attitudes all having a part to play. As for the future, there is still a great deal of work to be done by everyone concerned with child health in the area of breast feeding. However the results of this retrospective study on the subject do indicate that breast feeding is becoming the more popular method of infant feeding once again. The Baby Friendly Initiative in health care facilities and the education of young men and women in basic child care and parenting skills, in the form of Business Technical Educational Courses, General National Vocational Qualification and City and Guild courses, will all help to influence the attitudes and intentions of prospective parents. The information received through the Children of the Nineties study about parents education and child care practices will help to evaluate that influence.

FOOTNOTES

1. R. A. Lawrence. *Breast feeding: A guide for the medical profession.* C.V. Mosby Co., 1980. p.3.
2. Ibid. p.5.
3. F. Truby King. *Feeding and Care of Baby.* Oxford University Press. 1937. p.13.
4. Ibid. p.13.
5. C. Webster. 'Hungry or Healthy?' *History Workshop Journal.* 1981. p.111–127.
6. Truby King. p.81.
7. Ibid. p.81.
8. B. Spock. *The Commonsense Book of Childcare.* 3rd Edition. 1957. p.67.
9. *The Motherhood Book.* Amalgamated Press. 1930s. p.122.
10. Nurse Crawford. *Mother.* May, 1951.
11. J. & E. Newsom. *Patterns of Infant Care in an Urban Community.* Pelican. 1964. p.32.
12. DHSS Report on Health and Social Subjects. 1974. p.24(6.1.2).

Sleep Tactics

A Cradle Song

Sweet dreams, form a shade
O'er my lovely infant's head,
Sweet dreams of pleasant streams
By happy silent moony beams.

Sweet sleep, with soft down
Weave thy brows an infant crown.
Sweet sleep, Angel mild,
Hover o'er my happy child.

Sweet smiles, in the night
Hover o'er my delight;
Sweet smiles, Mother's smiles,
All the live long night beguiles.

From *Songs of Innocence* William Blake (1757-1827)

There is nothing quite like the sight of a baby sleeping, peaceful, innocent and trusting to bring a smile to our faces and a warmth to our hearts. There is nothing quite like the exhaustion of continually interrupted sleep or even no sleep at all to drive us to total distraction and despair. A baby that does not sleep at night is a very daunting prospect for even the most loving, patient and placid of parents.

Babies who do not sleep at night tend to be labelled as 'bad' babies, and those who do sleep at night are therefore 'good' babies. Authors like Truby King implied that 'bad' babies have 'bad' mothers! Thankfully the idea that babies are 'good' or 'bad' is now outdated – as far as the medical profession is concerned.

The question of sleep in babies is not really so much about the amount of sleep they should have but rather when they should have it. To 'fit in' with our society – we are not naturally nocturnal animals – ideally babies should sleep at night. However, as countless numbers of parents know, babies will not always conform to our habits. In this study, regardless of the decade in which they were born, approximately one third of all babies were poor night sleepers: a mixture of night wakers and those who just would not go to sleep at night at all!

Sleep has always been a major issue for parents and a wide range of advice has been given over the years to tackle the problem, ranging from where the baby should sleep – 'never take the baby to your bed' – to advice on 'spoiling' – 'leave the baby to cry it out.'

For Truby King, sleep followed the same strict, clock-watching discipline as every other aspect of a baby's routine. During the day the baby was to be fed, changed, put out to air and expected to sleep until its next feed time. However, a Truby King baby was never fed at night. The five feeds it received throughout the day were apparently quite sufficient. At the fifth feed (10 pm), the baby was to be handled quietly and not played with at all as this led to an excited baby who would not want to sleep. The baby was then put to bed and slept peacefully for eight hours, and he was to be woken at 6 am for his next feed. If a mother followed this schedule there was no reason for the baby to wake up at all during the night. Truby King allowed three reasons for night waking or crying:

1. Reflex – exercising the lungs.
2. Pain.
3. Attention seeking.

Thirst or hunger was not a possibility. Mothers were allowed to attend to their babies and change them if necessary but giving a feed was absolutely out of the question:

'There is no surer way of ruining a baby's digestion and converting him to a fretful, exacting little tyrant, who knows he can get his way by merely crying.'[1]

Truby King did not blame the baby for night waking; he laid the blame directly on the mother – 'a healthy baby with disturbed sleep is badly trained or spoiled'. Advice for mothers about what to do to 'unspoil' their night waker was rather negative – never take the baby into your own bed; the use of 'dummies' was deplored, rocking and cuddling, even the last resort of medication was strongly advised against. Other than changing a nappy the only recourse was to be firm and leave the baby to cry it out – a few nights of this and any baby would get the message – but there is no mention of ear plugs for frantic parents and neighbours!

The reasons for not taking a baby into your bed were longstanding. There was a strong fear of smothering or 'overlying' the baby, although this was, and is, an extremely rare occurence. The other reason Truby King puts forward is that the baby would be 'poisoned' by breathing in the mother's exhaled breath. Dr. Jolly disagreed and in the 1970s and 80s it became fashionable to allow your baby to sleep in your bed. This encouraged 'bonding', not only between the baby and his mother but with his father as well. A totally new phenomenon. Richards acknowledges the debate on where a baby should sleep but offers no opinion: 'this is another point where conflicts of interest occur and everyone needs to make their own choices'.[2] The main reason given for not taking a baby into your bed to sleep is that it can be extremely difficult to get him out again! Today the advice is not so didactic on the subject, but caution is still advised: 'If you let your child come in your bed, he will want to do it every night. So ask yourself if this is what you want.'[3]

As cuddling up in bed was seriously frowned upon, mothers looked to other sources of comfort, like the dummy. According to Truby King a dummy would deform the jaws, the teeth and palate, increase saliva and enlarge the adenoids, and was therefore to be avoided. By the 1950s, as child psychology became fashionable, so did dummies or 'pacifiers'. They were definitely thought preferable to the dreaded habit of thumb-sucking as a source of comfort, and they were popular in the treatment of colic and, it was felt, deformed the teeth much less than prolonged thumb-sucking would. One of the main concerns

19

about dummies in the past had been that they were unhygienic and dirty and also that they detracted from a baby's appearance; they were also disliked as a source of 'easy pleasure'. Dr. Spock advised that if the sight of a baby with a dummy in his mouth disgusted a mother then she should not allow its use. However if it is only the neighbours who are complaining a mother should tell them 'it is a very modern practice (or tell them that this is your baby)'. 45% of mothers in the Children of the Nineties study give their babies a dummy either at night, during the day or both.

On the amount of sleep that a baby should have Dr. Spock disregards the 18–20 hours that his predecessors cited. He simply states that 'one baby seems to need a lot, and another surprisingly little. As long as a baby is satisfied . . . you can leave it to him to take the amount of sleep he needs.'[4]

Not only had the strict rule book of the 1930s and '40s been undermined and parents given more choice and more confidence in their abilities to make those choices, but babies themselves were emerging as individuals who also had choices. The title Christina Hardyment chose for her chapter on *Dream Babies* of 1946–1981 was 'Baby Rules, O.K', indicating the shift in attitudes towards baby care. That shift was the very stuff that a Truby King 'exacting little tyrant' nightmare was made of!

Dr. Spock did allow a night feed for the first few weeks of life but a baby who would not sleep was again subjected to the firm handling techniques of Truby King: let the baby cry and do not go in to him at all.

The baby who would not 'go down' in the first place was to be taken to bed at a reasonable hour, parents were to say goodnight affectionately but firmly, walk out of the room and not go back. The habit of not going down, Spock assured, would be broken in three days. The golden, unbreakable rule was still firmly in place, even the permissive Dr. Spock could not recommend allowing a baby to sleep in the same bed as his parents.

Dr. Gibbens followed this advice into the 1960s. He expands the 'babies are individuals with individual needs' theory by stating that 'sleep depends on many things – on the baby's temperament, his management, his personal comfort, a sound digestion, fresh air and exercise, and his general health'.[5] He spoils this somewhat reasonable start by listing the different types of baby with different types of sleep pattern. Fat, placid and contented babies are heavy sleepers; thin and restless babies are light sleepers who are difficult to train and then there are 'normal' babies who settle to a regular sleep pattern with 'a little firm handling'.

Dr. Gibben's firm handling consisted of much the same as Truby King's and Spock's. Dr. Gibbens allowed a night feed but again strongly recommended a room of the baby's own as soon as possible and no bringing him into your bed. For the baby who would not go down immediately a mother should 'Put him down every evening at 6.30 pm and make up your mind not to go back to him.'[6] For the night waker, if firm handling failed 'a week or two in the country (with or without the baby?) or a sedative at night for a few weeks may tide you over the crisis' which he allows is a 'formidable' one!

For those parents who did not have access to a country cottage the permission to use a sedative was welcoming. One of the mothers in the Yesterday, Today . . . Tomorrow study stated that Vallergan was her 'crisis therapy' and was actually better than two weeks in Bermuda – so perhaps Dr. Gibbens was not so far off the mark!

The recommendation of a sedative marked a new trend in sleep tactics at this time. The Illingworths felt that Chloral was the best drug to use, suggesting that it was 'safest and it always works if given in sufficient dosage. This [the dosage] has to be determined by trial and error.'[7]

Sleep position is given some attention by Dr. Spock, in his revised version of *Baby and Child Care* 1957:

'I think it is preferable to accustom a baby to sleeping on his stomach from the start if he is willing'.[8]

'If he is willing' illustrates the new concept that a baby is capable of choice. However, Dr. Spock felt that babies preferred to sleep on their

tummies. It was a natural position for them. He gives two reasons why it was not advisable for a baby to sleep on his back:

1. Inhalation of vomit.
2. Distortion of the shape of the head – although he says this will not damage the brain and can be avoided by placing the baby at alternate ends of the cot at each sleep time, so that the 'distortion' is uniform!

Stomach sleeping was also the position recommended by the Illingworths in the 1960s:

'Many babies and small children sleep on their tummies. This is harmless providing they have no pillow and the mattress is firm, and it is probably a position to encourage. Babies sleep more if placed on the abdomen, they cry less and

22

it is safer for them, because if they are sick they are less likely to inhale vomit than if they are lying on their back.'[9]

In the Yesterday, Today . . . Tomorrow study the question was asked 'what position did you usually put your babies 'down' in?' The following figures give the results and suggests that Bristol mothers of the 1950s and '60s compromised between front and back sleeping position and placed their babies on their sides. It is in the 1970s that prone (front) sleeping became very popular.

As stated earlier advice on sleep position has changed dramatically in recent years. It is now considered dangerous to place a baby on his tummy to sleep. The preferred position is on his back or side. The results from the Children of the Nineties study show that this advice has been taken very much to heart by mothers in the Avon area. The national advertising campaign in October/November 1991 that followed the sad death of Ann Diamond's son has had a major effect on this aspect of infant care practice. This in turn appears to have had a major effect on the rate of Cot Death in this country, which has declined dramatically. Although it cannot be proved that sleep position is a cause of cot death, it certainly looks as though it is a contributory factor.

23

Sleep Position 1950 - 1990

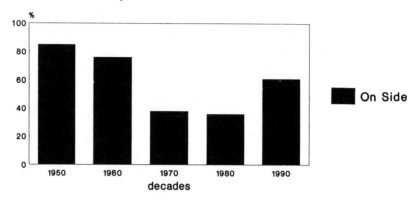

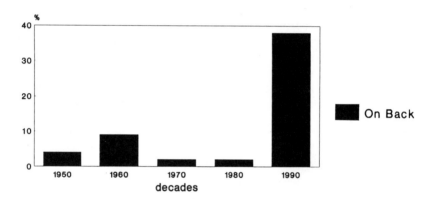

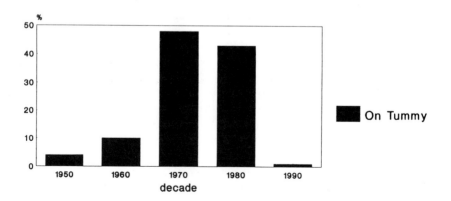

Like Spock and Gibbens, Jolly (1980) decided a baby should have no fixed amount of sleep. However it seemed to him that brighter babies needed less sleep than those who were not so bright. It was not babies who had sleep problems: it was their parents. Richards (1980) makes the point that sleep problems stem from the 'personality type' of the baby and not mismanagement by the parents. Whether or not parents found this reassuring is not known – parental practices can after all be adjusted, adjusting a personality type seems a far more daunting prospect! The baby care 'experts' seem determined to label babies one way or another. Instead of plain 'good' or 'bad' we now have 'personality types'; 'bright' and 'not so bright'; fat and content; thin and restless; the 'normal' baby is not easy to find.

Leach decided that sleep should not be a problem at all in her work *Babyhood*, 1974. If sleep *was* a problem it was because it interrupted valuable development time during the day. The trick was to keep your baby awake during the day and then night sleeping would not be a problem and maximum development would be gained. For the baby who did not sleep at night, she trod a middle line between the 'leave him to cry it out alone' school of thought and the 'spoiling' back to sleep tactic. She advised that you should go in to see your baby every five minutes to reassure him of your presence until the crying stopped. This advice can be found in today's advisory leaflets as well. You didn't 'coddle' your baby but you didn't have to listen to the agonising crying and do nothing.

A common problem for both babies and parents is the dreaded three month colic. Colic has a somewhat confusing history. There have been many schools of thought, ranging from the 'it does not exist' to the 'grin and bear it' brigades. Neither is particularly helpful when a baby is screaming inconsolably with his knees drawn up into his chest every evening for weeks on end! A colicky baby was often thought to be an attention seeker – though few would now agree with Bruce who, in 1961, in the *British Medical Journal*, labelled a baby suffering from colic as 'a malingerer'. Those who accept the existence of colic as a clinical condition still have problems agreeing its cause.

Spock (1957) disregards method of feeding as a cause. Breast milk, cow's milk and all kinds of formulas and fruit drinks can result in a colicky baby. Although acknowledging that the cause is unknown he suggests that it could be due to the baby's immature nervous system. In other words these babies are 'highly strung', need very gentle handling and should not be excited in any way.

Jolly (1980) suspected 'tension in the mother rather than a digestive problem in the baby'. Indeed it has been noted that if a baby with colic is admitted to hospital and removed from the vicious circle of frantic mother and distraught baby then the colic disappears. This view – that colic is the result of anxiety in the mother – remains popular. The Illingworths (1964) saw it differently, arguing that an anxious mother is the result of colic not the cause. Leach (1974) offered a little in the way of practical help, advising the mother to get her rest where she could and accept that she would have many sleepless and traumatic nights with her 'colicky' baby.

The hero of the piece was seen to be gripe water – in all its forms. In the 1950s and '60s it was given regularly after each feed as a preventative measure. It became a less popular practice in the 1970s and '80s, its use limited to when it was needed. An aspect of gripe water that was probably of most use in aiding a baby's sleep was the alcohol content. It was never thought of as a drug as such and its use was widespread as a 'cure-all' for generations. Although still used, it has not contained alcohol since the late 1980s.

Today the general consensus is that anything that works in getting your baby to sleep is acceptable – including the use of sedatives. There have also been some novel 'inventions' such as tape recordings of vacuum cleaners (apparently cylinder models are more effective than uprights in their ability to get babies to sleep). Tape recordings of sounds of the womb or the sea are also popular. Rocking, patting, singing, feeding, cuddling, taking out for a ride in the car, dummies, soft toys, sedatives, sleeping with the baby – all these things are now acceptable as ways of soothing a baby to sleep. Some parents still leave

their babies to 'cry it out' as a very last resort, when all else has failed and when their own levels of exhaustion are just too great. However the length of time that a baby is left to cry before receiving attention has declined greatly. In the 1950s, 53% of the study babies were left for between five and 10 minutes before a parent went to see what was wrong; by the 1980s this figure was down to 31%. It appears that in the past the message was 'leave him to cry' first and the idea that babies could be 'spoiled' and often cried for attention was very popular. Today the 'leave him to cry it out' solution is last on the list. It is now believed that babies cry for a reason and that it is the parent's responsibility to find that reason and attend to it. There is also a great deal more recognition that sleepless babies are a very serious problem for their parents, who therefore need sound advice and support. This is reflected in the setting up of helplines such as 'Cry-sis' and 'Parentline', where the essential message is 'Don't get desperate – get help'.

FOOTNOTES

1. Truby King. p.184.
2. M. Richards. *Infancy: World of the Newborn.* Harper & Row. London. 1980. p.43.
3. Health Visitors Association. *Encouraging Good Sleep Habits in Your Baby and Toddler.*
4. Spock, p.162.
5. J. Gibbens. *Care of your Young Baby.* J. & A. Churchill. London. 1962. p.131.
6. Ibid. p.131.
7. R. & C. Illingworth. *Babies and Young Children: A guide for parents.* 7th Edition. 1977. p.173.
8. Spock. p.163.
9. Illingworth. 3rd Edition. 1964. p.207.

The First Intruder . . .

'I can't think what fathers were invented for.'
Helen Maltus. Coming Thro' the Rye. 1880.

There have been many theories over the years about what a father's role actually is. Historical accounts tend to produce a stereotype based on traditional views. Today it is widely assumed that fathers are more involved in the practical and emotional care of their children. The main assumption is that fatherhood is a recent invention, a side effect of 'new man'. In this part of the Yesterday, Today . . . Tomorrow study we have followed the same pattern as many other researchers by asking women about men. How women perceive the men in their lives and their participation in caring for their children has an important impact on just how those men do care for their children.

While there is less research material available on the subject of fathers than mothers, recent work published by Lewis, Richman, O'Brien and McKee (1986, 1980, 1982, 1987) suggests that fatherhood has not been totally devoid of attention.

If you want answers to specific questions you should generally ask the people who are the subject of the research. However, in the study of fathers it has often been the case that the questions have been asked of mothers and taken as the last word. Mothers have never had their authority on the subject of fathers questioned. There are acceptable reasons for this. Just as until recent times male dominance of society has been the assumed 'norm', so too has the female dominance of child care. Also on a purely practical note, mothers are often more accessible to researchers, more likely to be at home during the day.

In 1951 Edith Buxbaum in a modern, permissive work for its time, *Your Child Makes Sense* stated that fathers were frequently absent and/or jealous of a new infant and were there to fulfil a masculine role-model only. She warned of grave danger in the role of the 'house husband' whose son would observe him pursuing 'feminine interests' of cooking and housework. She went on to give dire case histories of psychologically disturbed children brought up by fathers!

In 1953 in *Child's World*, Phyllis Hostler described the father as 'the first intruder' into the 'magic circle' of mother and child. Although a text book for fathers by English and Foster did exist in 1953, it was something of a lone voice.

In general the view of the division of labour in the parenting stakes remained 'involved' motherhood and 'supportive' fatherhood. Bowlby, in 1954, saw the mother as the key carer in infant rearing and the father was very much in the background. Expectations of a father were also far less than those of a mother. A father was an 'emergency' carer, someone to take over when a mother was unavailable and therefore was allowed to 'muddle through'. In other words mothers were mothers and fathers were babysitters. Although the Illingworths declare that the father has a big part to play in the practical care of the baby 'It goes without saying', they advise:

'He should be left to do it without a lot of criticism of his methods. The vest may be inside out, but the baby will not be harmed thereby.'[1]

The rest of the advice on the 'big part' that a father has to play is confined to one page!

Seel (1987) argues that in the 1950s there were clearly defined, socially acceptable roles for mothers and fathers. When a woman had a baby she became a mother. It was clear and simple. Fathers, however, had – and still have – no such biological bond. To mother is to be a source of comfort, nurture and love, there is a continuing relationship, an effort and commitment over time. To father however, is a single act with little effort and certainly no compulsory long term commitment. Fatherhood is not a biological fact in the same sense as motherhood, but a relationship that must be created. In most cases that relationship is created under the watchful eye of the mother and with divorced or unmarried fathers it is often controlled by mothers. This is a complete reversal since the last century, when a divorced woman was often the absent parent with custody being granted to fathers and women were often refused any access to their children. The changes in divorce law now leave many fathers in a delicate position, as is highlighted by the founding of groups such as 'Families Need Fathers'. However Seel argues that even for those fathers who remain within the family unit the extent of their involvement with their children is controlled by the mother. Richman in 1975 suggested that there is a 'cultural conspiracy' against fatherhood.

The Newsoms' study mentioned earlier in this book did produce some results on the practical involvement of fathers with their infants. As is usual the questions were asked of mothers. They categorised involvement (not including play, as it was taken for granted that the vast majority of fathers played with their children) as 'highly participant – will do anything; moderately participant – will do anything if asked; and non-participant – that's not a man's job'; The results were 52%, 27% and 21% respectively, with bathing the baby the least likely job a father would perform. The reasons put forward for this consisted mainly of some fear of hurting, dropping or drowning the baby on both the father's and the mother's part! Lewis undertook a study of 100 fathers of first and second born children in the same study area some 17 years later in 1979. He categorised in a similar way and found that 44% of the fathers in his study group were high participators, 44% were moderate and only 5% were non-participating in the practical care of their infants. Once again bathing the baby was the job a father was least likely to do. The YTT study revealed however that bathing the baby is a job that fathers have increasingly warmed to. In the Children of the Nineties study we have found that 32% of fathers bath their babies often and 29% do so occasionally. Play is excluded from the list of activities we suggested that fathers may do with their babies, as it has been assumed that this is the most common form of activity a father undertakes with his child. With the exclusion of play bathing emerges as the 2nd most popular activity!

ACTIVITY	YES OFTEN	YES OCCASIONALLY	HARDLY EVER
	%	%	%
Feeding	39	45	13
Bathing	32	29	35
Walking	21	44	32

Fathers' participation in practical baby care tasks. 1990s.

Brian Jackson undertook research on the subject of fathers in 1984. His study, based in Bristol, found that existing literature was largely limited to abnormal fathers – fathers who were absent from the home through divorce, imprisonment, death or mental illness. Little had been said about the normal, everyday Dad, who as far as the literature available was concerned seemed to be an invisible figure. Therefore he chose to study 100 first-time fathers who had normal, healthy babies and were in stable relationships. One of the first things he noticed was the confusion of mothers who wondered why on earth anyone would want to talk to the fathers of their children! This he attributed to a 'cultural incomprehension' rather than a 'conspiracy'. However by the early 1980s rising unemployment had changed the traditional pattern of man plus work equals mother and child. Large numbers of men were spending more time with their children even if it was forced through unemployment. Jackson asked 'Did men actually want to spend more time with their children and less time at work?' The national study in 1970 (CHES) had found that 40% of men came home to a sleeping child and amongst that group 11% were not there at the weekend either; consequently time, irrespective of quality of contact, was severely limiting in the building of paternal relationships. Jackson achieved a 100% response rate in his study, which he attributed to the novelty value of the study itself. He found that there was not only an overall increase in paternal involvement with infant care in comparison to previous studies, but an increase in the desire to be involved. However, this change had not occurred through education and one conclusion that Jackson came to was that there should be much better provision for educating young people in the art of parenting. Interestingly he also felt that men must become more aware of their emotional needs, echoing the feminist cries of the 1970s that women must become more aware of theirs. Men must assert their own feelings of tenderness without fear of losing their masculinity if they were to achieve closer relationships and involvement with their children: 'To release the full force of fatherhood will mean breaking the masculine taboo on tenderness.'[2]

McKee and O'Brien (1982) in their work *The Father Figure*, suggest that an effort should be made to promote 'bonding' between fathers and infants. They thought that the more frequent and immediate the contact between father and infant at birth the closer the ensuing involvement and tenderness. Just as 'bonding' became fashionable in the 1970s for mothers so too should fathers be encouraged to release their inner 'caring mechanisms'. Fathers attending the birth of their babies in this study went from 8% in the 1950s to 88% in the 1980s and now stands at 91%. Whether this has had the effect of 'bonding' fathers to their children has not yet been assessed.

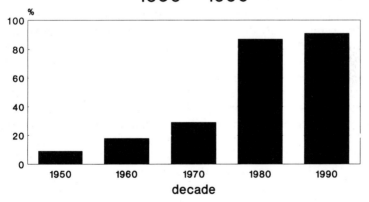

Father attending birth
1950 - 1990

Contemporary researchers of this topic, such as Lewis and O'Brien, are rather guarded on whether paternal involvement has actually increased or whether it is a result of increased research. There appears to be an assumption in society that fathers are now more involved with their children. In this study comments made by the mothers in each decade infer that one of the main changes in infant care practice is that fathers are now seen to be far more involved.

'Husbands are now much more involved with the day to day care.'
'Fathers generally have become much more involved with the birth and care of babies.'
'Husbands much more involved in all aspects.'
      Study mothers – Yesterday, Today . . . Tomorrow.
A general assumption such as this can alter the comments of the study population.

One of the things that complicate the assessment of paternal involvement with babies is the change in family and work patterns in society since the Second World War, especially the effect of maternal employment and paternal unemployment. Maternal employment has been the subject of much debate in recent years, mainly for its effect on children. In this study we can see the rate of paternal involvement with infants has risen faster than maternal employment levels:

Maternal Working
Paternal Involvement

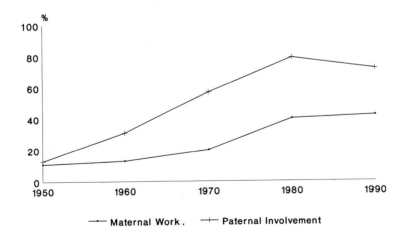

— Maternal Work.   —+— Paternal Involvement

33

The rise of maternal employment rates from the 1970s onwards could be seen as a result of the first stirrings of the feminist movement in Britain. More women began to return to work after childbirth, forcing a change in the division of labour within the home, although baby care was often the province of a female child minder or relative rather than the father. Nevertheless there is an increase in paternal involvement, defined by participation in practical infant care tasks with first-born children, from 57% in the 1970s rising to 79% in the 1980s.

It is tempting to associate this increase with the increase in paternal unemployment and more women becoming the main bread winner in the family. If we take this view then the concept of the 'new father' could be illusory. Increased paternal involvement could stem purely from financial necessity rather than any great shift in the emotional needs of men to be closely involved with their offspring.

This is something that Brian Jackson questions in his study of Bristol fathers in 1984: whether their increased involvement with their children is forced or voluntary. Seel argues in his work *The Uncertain Father* that men were driven to a more active role in the home by guilt.

Some feminists have seen the move towards paternal involvement in the home as just another way for men to exert power over women. Not content with browbeating women in the market place they (men) were now trying it in the field of child care – traditionally an area of female dominance. There seems to be a contradiction in terms with that argument. Women fought to get out of the restrictions that motherhood placed on them – such as the loss of continuity of employment or career prospects – but resent the increased involvement of fathers at the same time. Paternal involvement can be seen as a part of the whole debate surrounding gender roles in society.

Of course another consideration is that there are now huge variations in family structures. The nuclear family unit – two parents, two children – is not necessarily the 'norm' any more. More and more families are headed by single parents, including single fathers.

To claim that fathers of the 1980s and '90s are 'new' fathers who have more involvement in the practical care of their babies is to assume that fathers in previous generations did not have such involvement. Certainly the baby care experts of the inter-war years paid very little attention to the role of the father. Truby King does not mention fathers at all in *Feeding and Care of Baby*. He gave mothers sole responsibility for their babies. It could be argued, however, that Truby King's outright omission of fathers was preferable to Bertrand Russell's comments in *Marriage and Morals* (1929):

'No doubt the ideal father is better than none but many
fathers are so far from ideal that their non-existence might
be a positive advantage to children.'[3]

Once again it was Dr. Spock to the rescue of parents in the 1950s.
Although he did not have a great deal to say about the role of the
father, he did acknowledge that they have one and tried to reassure
them of it. 'The father is apt to get the idea that he's unimportant.'[4]
He went on to tell fathers that they could be 'a warm father and a real
man at the same time'. He encouraged fathers to take an active part in
caring for their baby. However equal shares is not quite what he had in
mind:

'Of course I don't mean that the father has to give just as
many bottles or change just as many diapers [nappies] as the
mother. But it is fine for him to do these things occasionally.'[5]

He suggests that the 2 am feed would be an ideal one for a father to
give. Hewlett's teething jelly manufacturers also assume that both
parents attend to their baby during the night, as seen in their 1951
advertisement in *Home Companion*.

The Browns are up again with their baby

It's always a disturbing and anxious time for everyone when
baby starts teething. But there's a way to ease baby's
fretfulness, sooth tender little gums and restore mother's
peace of mind, and that's with Hewlett's Teething Jelly.
Applied with finger direct to gums, it reduces soreness and
inflammation at once. Hewlett's is the ONLY teething
preparation in jelly form and its beneficial effects have won
wide clinical approval.

HEWLETT'S
Honey-Sweet
TEETHING JELLY

Obtainable from
chemists everywhere in
hygienic tube form,
price 1 10, including
P.T. Made by Hewlett's,
manufacturers of fine
Pharmaceutical pro-
ducts since 1832.

Although the father's role was finally being acknowledged both by the 'experts' and the media in the 1950s, it was thought that the creation of an 'involved' father was the responsibility of the mother. David Mace wrote a series of articles for *Woman* magazine in 1951 on the subject of marriage. In 'Baby Brings A Crisis', his advice to new mothers was:

> 'Nature does not implant in the father the same blind devotion to the baby as it does in the mother. Every man is not by instinct a parent. Fatherhood is something he has to grow into – and sometimes he needs help. . . . What women need to be taught is that . . . the wife must take upon herself the task of making her husband into a father.'[6]

The actress Googie Withers appears to be doing just that in an article in the *Home Companion*, April 1951.

Joanna seems quite unconcerned about Dad's attempts to fix her napkin, but Mother isn't quite so confident. Googie Withers and husband John McCallum with their baby daughter, Joanna.

By 1964 Dr. Gibbens devotes a whole chapter to the role of the father. He is very keen that a couple should 'run the baby together'. 'A baby is a joint concern, and every wife appreciates a husband who shares in the upbringing of HER child.'[7] I have emphasised the possessive 'her'. The chief role of the father was still that of provider, though – Dr. Gibbens advises a keen interest in the garden so that he (Dad) can supply his wife and baby with fresh vegetables; a stern line of defence where interfering relatives are concerned; unstinting support of his wife (even when she is wrong!) and the chapter ends with a recommendation of an insurance policy for the child, to assure its financial future or school fees!

Fathers' Involvement
Decades 1950 - 1990

Put To Bed

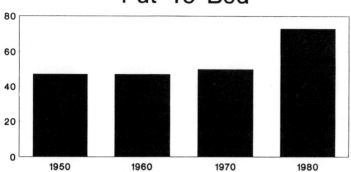

Walking

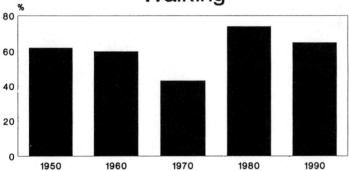

Feeding

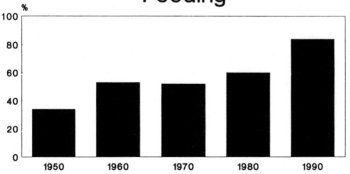

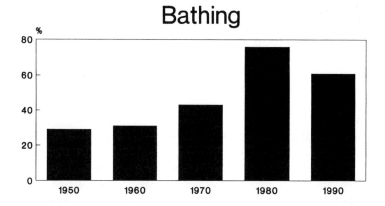

Bathing

The Newsoms decided from their findings in 1963 that 'the emancipation of women in one generation has led to the domestication of men in the next'.

Another aspect of the increase in paternal involvement is illustrated by the appearance at antenatal clinics of leaflets (and fathers!). The leaflets have titles such as 'It's Your Baby Too' and 'Becoming a Father'. The medical profession began speaking directly to men about the role of fatherhood and not to men through women.

In the 1990s the Children of the Nineties study has 9% house husbands who are the main carers for their babies and 72% of fathers who take an active role in the practical care of their baby. The graphs show the increase since 1950 in the number of fathers involved in the practical tasks of looking after their infants (who put the baby to bed was not asked of the 1990s mothers).

A straightforward frequency analysis of the data collected for this study reveals a definite and dramatic increase in paternal involvement since the 1950s. As discussed above there are a great many possible reasons for this. It seems likely that Brian Jackson's 'masculine taboo on tenderness', if not actually broken, has perhaps been dented a little.

FOOTNOTES

1. Illingworth. 3rd Ed. 1964. p.136.
2. B. Jackson. *Fatherhood*. Allen & Unwin. London. 1984. p.135.
3. B. Russell. *Marriage & Morals*. 1929.
4. Spock. p.16.
5. Spock. p.18.
6. *Woman*. May 1951.
7. Gibbens. p.20.

Vaccination

The medical profession are very clear and consistent on the subject of vaccination – unless there are medical indications not to vaccinate, such as a history of illness or previous reaction to vaccination, then all babies should be vaccinated against infectious disease. Not only does vaccination safeguard the individual child but, if sufficient numbers are vaccinated (90%), the whole community will also be protected.

The idea of individual responsibility for the health of the community as a whole has its roots in the eighteenth century. Infectious diseases of epidemic proportions have raged throughout the world since records began. Bubonic plague swept the country in the sixteenth and seventeenth centuries, and more recently smallpox, typhus and cholera accounted for many deaths in the eighteenth and nineteenth centuries. These diseases are no longer common and we rarely think of them unless travelling abroad. The last outbreak of bubonic plague was in the mid seventeenth century, smallpox is now officially eradicated from the world as a result of vaccination, and typhus and cholera are generally only found nowadays in countries with poor sanitary conditions.

The middle of the nineteenth century saw hospitals open all over the country specifically for the treatment of children. Bristol opened a hospital for children in 1866 and in the admission rules any child thought to be suffering from an infectious disease was not to be admitted. This measure was not as harsh as it sounds, Bristol Children's Hospital had the lowest mortality rate of all the children's hospitals in the country and wished to stay that way. Plans were being made to accommodate fever patients.

> 'The pressing demand is for a FEVER WARD, and for this object, special contributions will be most thankfully received. Many cases are constantly presenting themselves which it seems almost cruel to refuse; but the Committee have felt it to be absolutely necessary for the general well-being of the inmates, to prohibit the introduction into the Hospital of any patients suffering from infectious or contagious disease.'[1]

By 1871 a separate ward was established for the treatment and isolation of infectious disease. In 1877 there was a major outbreak of measles in the city and mortality was high.

When the new hospital was opened in St. Michaels Hill in 1885 a ward of four beds was allocated for children with measles and mothers

A ward in the Children's Hospital in the late nineteenth century.

who deliberately exposed their children to the disease were liable to be prosecuted for neglect.

Over the years Bristol has suffered regular outbreaks of measles. The Report from the City's Medical Officer in 1961 stated that there had been 8,682 reported cases and one death from the disease. A vaccine against measles was not introduced until 1968, although trials had been conducted in the city since 1965 with 'extremely promising' results, according to Dr. Wofinden, Medical Officer for Health.

The uptake of vaccinations available – diphtheria, tetanus and whooping cough (DPT) and polio – was reasonable at 87% for DPT and 65% for polio, according to Dr. Wofinden. Only one case of polio was reported in 1961. Vaccination against diphtheria had been successful and no cases had been reported since 1948. The new measles vaccine was received by 37% of the Yesterday, Today . . . Tomorrow study children of the 1960s, rising to 72% in the 1970s. The following graphs show the uptake of all the standard infant vaccinations received over the study period.

Whooping cough vaccine was surrounded by controversy in the 1970s and this is reflected in the uptake of vaccinations in the Yesterday, Today . . . Tomorrow study group – 84% of first-born study children in the 1960s, 71% 1970s and 90% 1980s. Although death from whooping cough is now thankfully much less likely, it remains a distressing illness which can leave a child with long term respiratory problems. Department of Health campaigns of the 1970s feature pictures of the distress whooping cough can cause.

Polio
1950 - 1990

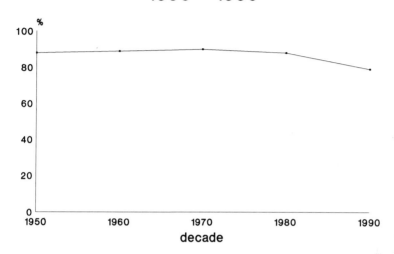

Measles
1950 - 1990

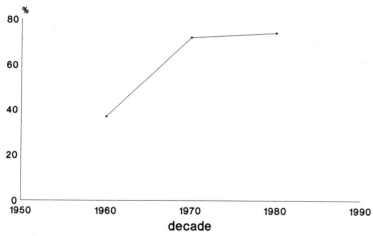

vaccine introduced 1968

Tuberculosis
1950 - 1990

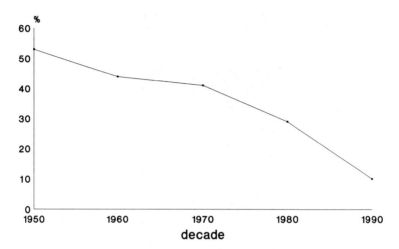

D.P.T.
1950 - 1990

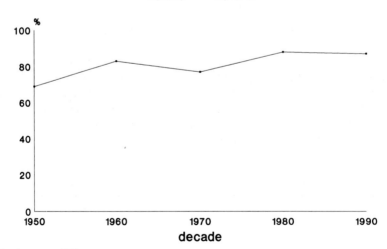

Vaccine scare 1970s

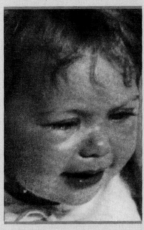

WHOOPING COUGH

Has your child been immunised?

*Ask your doctor or health visitor for
information about immunisation*

One aspect of vaccination that the medical profession differs about is exactly when vaccination should take place for maximum effect. This has changed quite recently and a new regime is now adhered to. In the case of whooping cough Dr. Huddy, writing for *Mother & Child* magazine in 1961, suggests that between 2–4 weeks of age is the time when children most need the protection of vaccination. He uses deaths from whooping cough over the period 1951–1959 in England and Wales to support his suggestion:

<3 months	3–5 months	6–8 months	9–11 months
286	274	178	133

Dr. Huddy's interpretation of the figures is that the older the infant when contracting the disease the less the likelihood of death, and therefore vaccination as early as possible would give maximum protection.

In 1977–79 Britain suffered an outbreak of whooping cough. The uptake of DPT (Triple) vaccine had dropped to 71% in the 1970s and community physicians feel that an uptake of 90% is needed for vaccination to be effective in the whole community. In 1978 the local evening paper, the *Evening Post*, carried a plea from the Medical Officer in Bristol for mothers to allow their children to be vaccinated. A few days later an article warns of 'Whooping Cough Epidemic' estimating a ten-fold increase in the number of cases:

'This highly contagious disease was rare until reports last year that whooping cough vaccinations could cause brain damage.'[2]

In 1980 the papers carried articles about alleged vaccine-caused brain damage. A mother whose first child was said to be vaccine-damaged after the whooping cough vaccination stated that she would rather nurse her second child through whooping cough than risk brain damage. In the same article a 'West Country Health Expert' stated 'there is no evidence of a link between the vaccine and brain damage', yet this mother received compensation for her child's injuries.

In 1989 there was another whooping cough alert. Whooping cough seems to peak every four years and in the winter of 1989/90 a peak was expected. The official figure of vaccine uptake at this time was 80%, good but not enough to prevent an outbreak of the disease. Parents were told:

'Treatment once you have it (whooping cough) is not very effective and the only thing you can really do is ensure children are vaccinated against it.'[3]

The article offered some figures to reassure parents. If vaccine damage occurs the risk is only 1:110,000 whilst death from the disease occurs in 1:45,000. Basically the child with whooping cough is over twice as likely to die as the child who has the vaccination is to be brain damaged. Research carried out at the Bristol Institute of Child Health has shown that whooping cough in a young infant can itself cause brain damage.

Polio vaccination has had a happier history and has been successful. Oral polio vaccination became available for general use in this country in the mid 1960s; in the 1950s and early '60s the vaccine was administered via injection. There was a national campaign to increase the uptake of polio vaccination in 1961. *Woman* magazine carried an article from Sister Williams. There had been an increase in the

Mother hits at vaccine claims

West parents in whooping cough alert

18 SEP 1989

By Vikki Orvice

...ORS ... are ...te parents to ...n. their ...g against ...ng cough ...s of a West

The infection ... which can kill — peaks every four years and health experts are predicting a dramatic ... the number of ... winter.

In Bristol alone there were 70 cases up to August compared to 33 for the same ...

23 SEP 1989 By ALLAN GUY

A MOTHER said ...
nurse he
than risk

Mrs Lesley
i. Quarry C
ear Dursle
:10,000 comp
er first child
ll after a wt
vaccination.

Mrs Gardner
another child
said today: "I
to take the ri:
a child throu
cough than :
cinated.

A West C
health expert
Freemans yes
a report whic
was no evid
whooping coug
brain damage.

But Mrs
today: "C h
damaged —
is proof."

Lee, now a:
a normal heal
he. develope
the day aft
cinated for, w
she said.

"He got o!
compared w
dren."

"I think it's up to par
to decide. Because I h
had one child damaged
am not going to
anything with the n
one."

Killer epidemic 'set to strike'

Heath.vacc.

14 OCT 1989

PARENTS BLAMED IN DISEASE ALERT

By Nigel Dando

AN epidemic of whooping cough is facing children in the Bath area because too few parents have had their youngsters immunised again.

The ...
poised
Too
unabl
Dis
nity
Len

definitely a chance that Bath could have an epidemic on its hands.

"Our immunisation uptake rate is 76 per cent, which is not enough to prevent epidemics. It

immunisation can lead to brain damage.

But Dr Lenton said: "It is a very small risk compared with the risk that children will come into contact with whooping cough." District immunisation

months and damage the lining of the lungs.

The last epidemic hit the Bath area three years ago when a baby died and 173 other cases were reported between January and October.

Doctors say only one in 110,000 immunised children ...ain damage. 3ritain's 1982 gh epidemic, one ungsters died

VOICE OF THE WEST TEMPLE WAY, BRISTOL, BS99 7HD EVENING POS

Parents should not be misled by homoeopaths

Whooping cough jabs DO protect your children

31 DEC 1985

AS PRESIDENT of the British Faculty of Homoeopathy I am concerned that misleading advice has discouraged some parents from letting their children have the conventional

Dr John Hughes-Games: concerned.

course of whooping cough injections (which are, in a sense, homoeopathic).

This advice often comes from homoeopaths who are not qualified in conventional medicine.

There is definite evidence that the conventional injection affords quite a high degree of protection and if the child should catch whooping cough it is likely to be less severe

if the course has been given.

We have no evidence that homoeopathic "immunisation" has any effect at all.

Modify

Those of us who use it have a clinical impression that it helps to prevent the illness or to modify it.

It is therefore most important that, unless there are individual medical reasons against it, the conven-

tional course of injections should be given.

Whooping cough is a very alarming and potentially dangerous illness particularly in young children.

If a parent is in doubt I beg them to discuss it with their general practitioner who is well informed about the matter.

Dr John Hughes-Games Whitchurch Health Centre, Armada Road, Whitchurch, Bristol.

45

numbers of polio cases reported in unvaccinated people. Sister Williams stated:

> 'Such a simple procedure; one prick, and that's that. Not much time lost in waiting. But match any inconvenience caused against the possible alternative. There is little doubt, is there, as to which is the best course for everyone.'[4]

The uptake of polio vaccination has been consistent throughout the study period at 88–92%.

Diphtheria vaccine was also the subject of a national campaign in the 1950s with advertisements appearing in popular magazines.

The latest vaccine to hit the headlines as having possibly dangerous side effects has been the new MMR (Measles, Mumps and Rubella). In 1989, the *Evening Post* carried an article about a child who became ill with 'meningitis-like' symptoms for eight months. Health experts denied any connection between the vaccine and the illness. The illness was nevertheless later diagnosed as 'Post-viral Syndrome caused by MMR vaccine'. In 1992 two brands of the vaccine were withdrawn in a blaze of publicity. The two brands accounted for 85% of all vaccinations and it had been found that there was indeed a connection with 'a mild form of meningitis'. The Department of Health 'hoped parents would not be discouraged from having their children vaccinated'.

Vaccination against fatal, infectious diseases can be argued to have been one of the greatest achievements of medicine and it is generally accepted as a sensible precaution. However, the anti-vaccinationists do have a voice and there is still an active group today. If public health is to be successfully protected by individual action then the reporting of 'vaccine scares' should perhaps be handled with more care. Vaccination is not compulsory. The idea of collective responsibility of a community toward each other is secondary to the concerns of parents about the individual benefit to their child. Media reporting of vaccine scares do seem to have an effect on the rate of uptake. Whooping cough notifications rise when vaccine uptake declines, usually in connection with a vaccine-damage scare as this study shows.

Note: Any parents who are considering vaccination for their child and have fears or worries should talk it over with their doctor or health visitor.

FOOTNOTES

1. Bristol Children's Hospital Report. 1867.
2. *Bristol Evening Post.* 1978.
3. *Western Daily Press.* 1989.
4. Sister Williams. *Woman.* 1961.

As well as any influence that a doctor, midwife or health visitor may have, a new mother also has her own parents and parents-in-law to lend a hand, or contend with, as the case may be!

A new grandchild is an exciting and wonderful prospect for most people. They have brought their own children up, now they can have real fun with their grandchildren and someone else can get out of bed for the 2am feed. The one thing you cannot escape about grandparents is that they are experienced parents and there is no substitute for experience! There is, though, a fine line between offering advice and support and taking over and interfering, as many grandparents have found.

This last chapter discusses some of the more obvious changes in baby care practice since the 1950s such as potty-training and daily airing. These were two aspects of baby care that were very firmly in place in the 1950s and have very definitely changed today.

Toilet-training is now usually begun in the second year of life but this has not always been so. A Truby King baby – if he had a well trained mother – was 'habit' trained by the age of two months.

Truby King approaches toilet-training with the same strict discipline that he approaches every other aspect of child care. Rule VIII (8) states:

> 'Try to get the bowels evacuated regularly at the same hour every day, regardless of whether there is any natural tendency or inclination for a motion at the appointed time or not.'[1]

If a 'natural tendency' is missing, he advocates the use of a mild salt water enema given with a soft, rubber catheter, although he is against the use of a soap stick as a stimulant!

The very idea of giving a perfectly healthy six week old baby any 'help' in evacuating his bowels purely for him to 'perform' at a set time is totally alien to today's mothers.

In fairness to Truby King he does use the term 'habit-training' and recognises it as such. It is now thought that most children do not develop a sense of needing to pass urine or empty their bowel until around 18 months – 2 years of age. Any success in getting children 'dry' and 'clean' or 'out of nappies' prior to that age is thought to be the result of good timing on the mother's/carer's behalf. In the Children of the Nineties study 2% of mothers state that they are potty-training their children before the age of one year. There is no documented

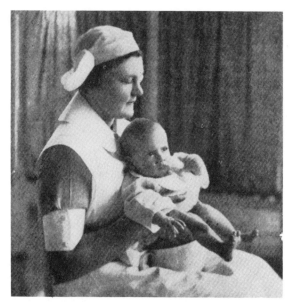

Trying to get the bowels evacuated regularly! From *Feeding and Care of Baby*, Truby King, OUP 1937.

evidence that either way is 'better' for the child or the mother.

Dr. Spock, as we have come to realise throughout this book, once again comes to the rescue, perhaps in the case of the baby this time, rather than the parent:

> 'It's fairly easy to catch the movements of a baby who is naturally regular, but he isn't really trained in his first year . . . It's his mother who is trained.'[2]
>
> 'The most that a mother needs to do is to watch her child . . . and give him some positive encouragement.'[3]
>
> 'It seems to me sensible to give the baby the benefit of the doubt and not fuss at him until he is old enough to understand a little better.'[4]

Even so 47% of the Yesterday, Today . . . Tomorrow study mothers were potty training their first-born children in the 1950s before the age of one year.

Dr. Gibbens has remarkably little to say on the subject of toilet-training during the 1960s. In fact he is positively permissive, in contrast to some of his other advice, allowing mothers to revert to nappies at the least sign of resistance and try again later.

The idea of 'forcing' a baby into a rigid regime of toilet-training before he is naturally ready for it was no longer recommended by the experts of the late 1950s onwards. Although the Newsoms' study of Nottingham mothers in 1963 revealed that 83% were still training their babies before the age of one year, in their later follow-up study of

Toilet training
1950 - 1990

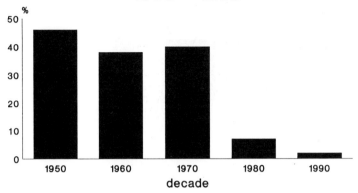

four year olds they found that the age at when training started could affect the continence of the four year olds but their findings were not conclusive. Amongst the Yesterday, Today . . . Tomorrow study mothers, in the 1960s only 38% were toilet-training before one year.

In 1974 Leach was placing toilet-training firmly as a matter of pride and convenience to the mother:

'He will pass a motion when he needs to and only his mother cares whether it goes in a pot or in his clothes.'[5]

'In practical terms, early potting seems a lot of effort for not much reward.'[6]

Richards continues to highlight the conflict between the baby's ability to understand the process of toilet-training and the parents desire for it to be achieved as soon as possible:

'Control of elimination is another ability which an infant can afford not to develop for the first couple of years despite what parents might sometimes feel about this.'[7]

The Well-Baby Book of 1979 suggests leaving toilet-training until the age of eighteen months and then to enhance voluntary control by pointing out wet or soiled nappies to the baby, to increase his awareness and if possible to leave training until the summer months when the baby has fewer clothes on.

On a nostalgic note the one thing about pre-disposable nappies that some of the Yesterday, Today . . . Tomorrow study mothers seemed to miss was the sight of a washing line full of white towelling nappies blowing in the wind on a crisp, sunny morning. Although it makes a very pleasant photograph I doubt whether there are many mothers who do not appreciate the freedom from nappy washing that disposables give.

One reason put forward in the textual answers from these mothers was the lack of automatic washing machines or twin-tubs to wash and boil their towelling nappies:

'I potty-trained much earlier than they do today, no doubt to save on nappy washing, we washed by hand and boiled them which took up such a lot of time.'

'There were no disposable nappies in my day, they must be a godsend, especially in bad weather.'

YTT Study Mothers.

Domestic Appliances
1950 - 1990

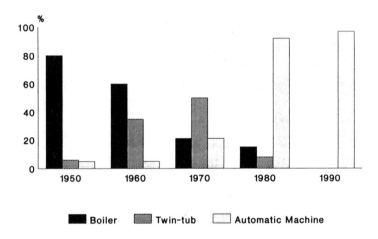

We asked about the domestic washing appliances mothers had in each decade, such as boiler, twin-tub, automatic washing machine. Regardless of whether disposable nappies are used rather than towelling ones, the mothers who gave birth in the 1980s were far more likely to have an automatic washing machine. As anyone who has ever used towelling nappies knows, they add considerably to the household wash load and prior to the age of the tumble dryer they also gave considerable drying problems.

As well as nappies being blown around in fresh air another practice that appears to have declined is putting babies 'out to air' on a daily basis. For Truby King an 'abundance of pure, cool, outside air flowing fresh and free day and night' is the first rule in his list of 'What Every

Baby Needs'. While stating that a baby must be properly clothed he tells us that 'Pure, cold air is invigorating, and prevents "catching cold"'. Not only this but:

> 'Properly fed babies who have plenty of open air and kicking exercise during the day, and pure, cool air at night, sleep like doormice and give their parents from six to eight hours uninterrupted rest.'[8]

Dr. Spock continues the theme that 'fresh air' is good for general health:

> 'It is good for a baby (like anyone else) to get outdoors for 2 or 3 hours a day, particularly during the season when the house is heated.'[9]

There is a little more detail in Dr. Spock's advice. He gives examples of how much fresh air and at what temperature an average ten pound baby should have, but in general all babies should be 'put out to air' as long as it was not raining and the temperature was above freezing. Even when the temperature was below freezing a 'twelve pound baby can be comfortable in a sunny sheltered spot for an hour or two'.

If you had no 'back yard' or garden in which to place your baby then you were to push him out in a carriage (pram). Another aspect of putting babies out to air was also to give them sun baths. Dr. Spock again: 'Direct sunshine contains ultraviolet rays, which create vitamin D right in the skin.'[10]

He does warn against sun burn and possible trouble with the eyes from too great an exposure.

99% of the mothers from the 1950s who took part in the Yesterday Today . . . Tomorrow study gave their babies a 'daily airing' or 'sunbath'. One reason for this – other than the benefit to the baby of the fresh air – was that the mother could then get on with organising her household chores, while the baby slept safely in the garden. It was very much a part of a fixed routine. By the 1960s, Dr. Gibbens was lamenting that 'many (mothers) will do little or nothing to see that they (babies) get enough fresh air'. He stated that a baby need only be indoors in foggy weather or when there is driving rain. 'Cold weather, even when there is snow on the ground, does a baby nothing but good as long as he is warmly dressed.'[11]

Throughout the 1960s this practice declined not so much because there was no longer a belief in the physical benefits of the practice, but because it was felt to be detrimental to the childs psychological development. Leaving a baby in a pram with 'nothing to do but a brick wall to see' was a very poor practice according to the Illingworths. There was now a push for a daily walk in the pram but more for the mother's benefit than the baby's. Prams have also undergone a revolution in the last forty years. The massive carriages of the 1950s ('We had real prams in my day' – study mother 1950s) have given way to lightweight, foldaway pushchairs and buggies. The baby-sling or carrier has also become popular. Oakley explains its popularity as something fathers feel more comfortable with – rather than pushing a pram. Richards also found the baby-sling a useful object for paternal

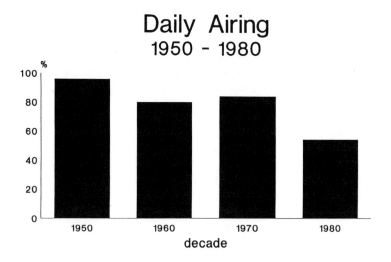

Daily Airing
1950 - 1980

bonding, allowing the father to keep the baby close to his body. The movement of the adult's body so close to the baby has a calming, reassuring effect that cannot be found when lying down in a pram or buggy.

Leach does not mention the subject of fresh air or sunbathing in her index to *Babyhood* 1974. However the 1970s saw an increase in environmental awareness in general and the quality of the air around us. The Control of Pollution Act was passed in 1974 and by the 1980s various government bodies had been set up to investigate the environment: Standing Royal Commission on Environmental Pollution; the Clean Air Council and the Advisory Council on Noise. There were also voluntary agencies such as the Keep Britain Tidy group and pressure groups such as Friends of the Earth.

In the YTT study 84% of mothers of the 1970s were still giving their babies a 'daily airing' – whether by walking out with them or placing them in the garden. By the 1980s this figure had declined to 52%. The term 'daily airing' was by then obsolete and therefore mothers from the 1980s did not make the connection between taking their baby out for a walk to the park in the pram and placing the baby in the garden for two hours. However more people had access to a vehicle by the 1980s and public transport was also more readily available so perhaps the daily walk had declined in favour of the outing in the car to the shops or to granny's house. Certainly from comments made by the Yesterday Today . . . Tomorrow study mothers it seems that the general impression is that mothers do not walk out with their babies any more:

'A lot of young mums don't take their babies out in the fresh
air for walks, it's always in the car from A to B.'
'Babies are taken everywhere in cars instead of walking.'
'Babies don't go for good walks any more.'
'Life was slower, you walked your baby rather than drove.'
Study Mothers – Yesterday, Today . . . Tomorrow

We did not ask whether our mothers had access to cars or use of public transport so we cannot clarify this assumption. However, there were many comments such as these and often in a nostalgic tone. One mother had no regrets for her 'old fashioned boiler' but was positively sentimental about her 'beautifully well sprung pram'.

Over the four decades we have found many things that have changed but few with any scientific justification. It seems that baby care practice is as subject to fashion as anything else and so are the 'experts'. Perhaps the important thing to realise is that there is no perfect recipe for the perfect baby. Advice is always useful. Even if rejected, it gives a different perspective on a problem. As with all things there are aspects of the past that can be brought into the present with positive effects and there are some things that should be left in their era. Baby care has changed considerably from the 1950s, there are more labour saving devices for the busy mum to use and there have been advances in our knowledge about how to care for babies.

The one thing that every mother in the study agreed upon was this: however we choose to care for our babies, whatever advice we accept or reject the thing that matters the most is that we care for our babies and children with love.

A great deal of infant care practice appears to have evolved through habit rather than any direct evidence of what is actually best for mothers, fathers or children. Most of Truby King's advice is now considered old-fashioned and has been abandoned, yet this has occured without any questions about whether the advice was good or bad. Children of the Nineties is ideally placed to assess the infant care practices that parents use today; to find out what results these practices have and find the ones that have the most beneficial effect. This will benefit the parents but most of all it will benefit the children of the next decades.

FOOTNOTES

1. Truby King. p.41.
2. Spock. p.245.
3. Ibid.
4. Ibid.
5. P. Leach. *Babyhood*. 1974. p.290.
6. Ibid.
7. Richards. p.53.
8. Truby King. p.46.
9. Spock. p.159.
10. Ibid. p.161.
11. Gibbens. p.129.

Bibliography

Blake W. *Songs of Innocence and Experience.*

Buxbaum E. *Your Child Makes Sense: A Guide for parents.* Allen & Unwin. London. 1951.

Cobb J. *Babyshock. A mother's first 5 years.* Arrow Books. London 1980.

Gallagher E. B. *Infants, Mothers and Doctors.* Lexington Books, Toronto. 1978.

Gibbens Dr. J. *The Care of Young Babies.* J & A Churchill. London 1962. 5th Edition.

The Glaxo Volume 8. Glaxo Labs. Middlesex. 1953.

Hostler P. *Child's World.* 1953.

Illingworth R & C. *Babies and Young Children: A guide for parents.* 3rd, 4th & 7th Editions. 1964, 1967, 1977.

Jackson B. *Fatherhood.* Allen & Unwin, London. 1984.

Jolly H. *Book of Child Care.* Sphere Books. 1977.

Lawrence R.A. *Breast feeding: A guide for the medical profession.* C.V. Mosby Co. 1980.

Leach P. *Babyhood.* Penguin. 1975.

Lewis C. *Becoming a Father.* Oxford University Press. 1986.

Lewis C. & O'Brien M. *Reassessing Fatherhood: New observations on fathers and the modern family.* Sage Publications. London. 1987.

Maltus H. *Coming Thro' the Rye.* 1880.

McKee L. & O'Brien M. *The Father Figure.* Tavistock Publications, London. 1982.

The Motherhood Book. Amalgamated Press. 1930s.

Newsom J. & E. *Patterns of Infant Care in an Urban Community.* Pelican. 1963.

Oakley A. *From Here to Maternity: Becoming a Mother.* Penguin. 1979.

Richards M. *Infancy: World of the newborn.* Harper & Row London. 1980.

Russell B. *Marriage & Morals.* 1929.

Seel R. *The Uncertain Father: Exploring modern fatherhood.* Gateway Books, Bath. 1987.

Spock Dr. B. *Commonsense Book of Childcare.* 1957. 3rd edition.

Stanway A. & P. *Breast is Best.* 1978.

Truby King Sir F. *Feeding and Care of Baby.* Oxford University Press. 1937.

Wallace W.H.S. *Infant and Child Care.* Cassell & Co, London. 1951.

The Well Baby Book. 1979.

JOURNALS:

1. Bristol Children's Hospital Annual Reports.
2. *Bristol Evening Post.*
3. DHSS Report on Health and Social Subjects. 1974.
4. Health Visitors Association. *Encouraging Good Sleep Habits in your Baby and Toddler.*

5. *History Workshop Journal.*
6. *Home Companion.*
7. *Midwifery Dialogue.*
8. *Mother.*
9. *Mother & Child.*
10. *People's Friend.*
11. Report of the Medical Officer for Health. 1951, 1961, 1971.
12. *Western Daily Press.*
13. *Woman.*